TAGORE

—

THE MYSTIC POETS

TAGORE

—

THE MYSTIC POETS

Translated from Bengali into English
by the author

Preface by Swami Adiswarananda,
Minister and Spiritual Leader of the
Ramakrishna-Vivekananda Center of New York;
author of *Meditation & Its Practices*

Walking Together, Finding the Way®
SKYLIGHT PATHS®
PUBLISHING

Tagore:
The Mystic Poets

2004 First Printing
© 2004 by SkyLight Paths Publishing

Library of Congress Cataloging-in-Publication Data
Tagore, Rabindranath, 1861–1941.
[Poems. English. Selections]
Tagore / translated from Bengali into English by the author;
preface by Swami Adiswarananda.
p. cm.—(The mystic poets series)
ISBN 978-1-59473-008-5 (hardcover)
ISBN 978-1-68336-325-5 (pbk.)
1. Tagore, Rabindranath, 1861–1941—Translations into English. 2. Tagore, Rabindranath, 1861–1941—Religion. 3. God in literature. I. Title. II. Series.
PK1722.A2T26 2004
891'.4414—dc22

2003024269

SkyLight Paths, "Walking Together, Finding the Way" and colophon are trademarks of LongHill Partners, Inc., registered in the U.S. Patent and Trademark Office.

Walking Together, Finding the Way

Published by SkyLight Paths Publishing
www.skylightpaths.com

Contents

Preface

Swami Adiswarananda

In his introduction to Tagore's *Gitanjali,* William Butler Yeats makes the following remark: "We write long books where no page perhaps has any quality to make writing a pleasure, being confident in some general design, just as we fight and make money and fill our heads with politics—all dull things in the doing—while Mr. Tagore, like the Indian civilization itself, has been content to discover the soul and surrender himself to its spontaneity."

An immensely versatile poet, novelist, essayist, playwright, composer, and artist, Rabindranath Tagore's presence is felt everywhere in India. *Gitanjali* ("Song Offerings"), a collection of poems for which he was awarded the Nobel Prize in Literature in 1913, was published in English translation in London the previous year. In the words of the Nobel Foundation, the award was given "because of his profoundly sensitive, fresh, and beautiful verse, by which, with consummate skill, he has made his poetic thought, expressed in his own English words, a part of the literature of the

1

West."

The fourteenth child of Devendranath Tagore, Rabindranath was born in Calcutta and wrote his first verse when he was eight. Quite early in his life he came under the influence of the Brahmo Samaj, the religious movement of which his father Devendranath Tagore was the leader. Devendranath introduced his son to the great religious literature of India—the Upanishads. Poetry was Rabindranath Tagore's life breath. His religion is the religion of a poet; Plato banished poets from his ideal republic, but to Tagore, poetry's mission is to occupy people's lives and not merely exist for scholarly enjoyment. With Tagore, the infinite becomes the finite without losing its infinity. The finite is the dynamic manifestation of the infinite. God, according to Tagore, is the Supreme Person seated in the hearts of all. The goal of spiritual quest is to become united with that infinite Person or God.

Tagore sees creation as the revelation of truth. His mystic mind gets absorbed in his Personal God and becomes an instrument in God's hands. The freedom-loving poet and mystic Tagore, with his spiritual vision, advocates a poet's religion that is all embracing and all loving.

Tagore had a deep regard for the nineteenth-century God-man and prophet of the harmony of faiths, Sri Ramakrishna (1836–1886), and his foremost disciple Swami Vivekananda (1863–1902). In his beautiful homage to Sri Ramakrishna Tagore writes:

> Diverse courses of worship
> from varied springs of fulfillment
> have mingled in your meditation.
> The manifold revelation of the joy of the Infinite
> has given form to a shrine of unity in your life.
> Where from far and near arrive salutations
> to which I join mine own.

In regard to Swami Vivekananda, Tagore told the noted French savant Romain Rolland, "If you want to know India, study Vivekananda" (quoted in *World Thinkers on Ramakrishna-Vivekananda*, edited by Swami Lokeswarananda, pp. 10, 34).

Rabindranath Tagore's philosophical and spiritual thoughts transcend all limits of language, culture, and nationality. In his writings, the poet and mystic Tagore takes us on a spiritual quest and gives us a glimpse of the infinite in the midst of the finite, unity at the heart of all diversity, and the Divine in all beings and things of the universe.

Swami Adiswarananda,
Ramakrishna-Vivekananda Center of New York

Who Is Rabindranath Tagore?

Rabindranath Tagore (1861–1941) is widely considered the greatest influence in modern Indian literature. In his native land of Bengal—which is known today as the country of Bangladesh—his influence is equal to that of Shakespeare throughout the English-speaking world. His songs are sung in elementary schools, and his poems and other writings are the subject of numerous theses and dissertations at the universities each year. Indians revere Tagore as an artist, sage, reformer, and spiritual leader; Tagore's work and life are the subject of frequent conferences and books that deal with what his vision might mean for the future of India.

He made a significant contribution to education, expanding his father's small school into a university and instituting reforms that are in place to this day; created a new form of Indian musical composition; founded an important ashram; became a vital conduit of Indian culture to the Western world at a time when Britain and India were warring with each other; and, late in life, while exploring his own emergence as a visual artist, introduced modern and abstract painting to his people. Tagore was innovative in writing his poetry in the vernacular Bengali language rather than in the traditional Sanskrit—thereby almost single-handedly creating what is now Bengali literature—and his poetry evokes the flavor of the real Indian countryside, not the Anglicized India of the colonial period.

Tagore's influence has also been felt around the world. His books have been translated into numerous languages, and his verse speaks to people from all backgrounds who seek a deeper understanding of self, country, creation, God, and love. People have hungered for Tagore's wisdom; in the last two decades of the Soviet Union, in the 1970s and 1980s, more than a million copies of his books were sold in translation, despite (or perhaps because of) their obvious spiritual themes.

His vast literary output, the remarkable diversity of his talents, and his wide range of personal influence made him perhaps the most important bridge between the spirituality of the East and the West in the first half of the twentieth century.

An accomplished poet, novelist, short story writer, painter, playwright, philosopher, and educator, Tagore first achieved fame in the West when he was awarded the Nobel Prize for Literature in 1913. The prize coincided with the publication in English of *Gitanjali* ("Song Offerings"), Tagore's most important collection of poems or songs up until that time and still his most-read work. Aided by his friendships with prominent literary figures in Britain and America, including William Butler Yeats and Ezra Pound, Tagore's influence grew rapidly. Like Eastern religious figures before him, such as Ramakrishna's student Vivekananda, who brought Indian religion to the great cities of Europe and North America two decades earlier, Tagore was viewed with both awe and suspicion in different areas of society. He rapidly became an Eastern mystic who commanded attention throughout the West, enjoying a worldwide reputation until his death at age eighty.

Tagore was already fifty-two years old by the time *Gitanjali* was published in Britain, but it seemed to many people in the West at that time that Tagore had suddenly appeared out of nowhere. *Gitanjali* was first published by Macmillan & Company in March 1913 and went through thirteen additional printings in that year alone, then thirty more printings before the end of the decade. Within a few years of his "bursting" on the scene in London, Tagore was awarded the British knighthood, but he later voluntarily surrendered it as a protest against the 1919 massacre at Amritsar in India, where British troops fired on unarmed Indians peacefully demonstrating against British colonial powers, killing almost four hundred people and leaving more than 1,000 wounded.

Many of Tagore's conversations with other luminaries of the early twentieth century were recorded and published, including his talks with Albert Einstein, Mahatma Gandhi, H. G. Wells, George Bernard Shaw, Thomas Mann, and Robert

Frost.

Tagore was born in Calcutta and later died there, but he traveled extensively around the world for all of his life. He was born into a wealthy and prominent Brahmin family. His grandfather was an industrialist and his father was a renowned scholar and religious reformer. Rabindranath once wrote: "[I have] been brought up in a family where texts of the Upanishads are used in daily worship; and [I have] had before [me] the example of [my] father, who lived his long life in the closest communion with God, while not neglecting his duties to the world, or allowing his keen interest in all human affairs to suffer any abatement" (*Sadhana*, p. vii).

The Tagores were one of the wealthiest and most influential families in all of India, and they were also one of the most artistically talented. Rabindranath was the youngest child, and he started to write poems at the young age of eight. His early education came from private tutors in the home, but later he attended Bengal Academy before leaving for London and University College. Tagore studied law in London, but he left within a year without earning a degree.

He was often critical of his own poems and always felt that his fame was unfortunate, for it took away from his ability to create the sort of poetry he truly wanted to create. Tagore usually translated his own poems from Bengali into English. They retain something of an exotic flavor, perhaps in part due to Tagore's relative unease with English phrasings and words. Also, Tagore's genius was to transmit the feeling of the real India, unadorned and uninfluenced by its colonial rulers and culture. His work is overwhelmingly mystical, fresh from the spirituality of India, but with none of the feel of the parish or pulpit so common in the religious poetry of England and America during the late nineteenth and early twentieth centuries. Tagore once remarked to Ezra Pound, the modernist poet, about the English translations of his poems:

> They have not been purposely made moral, they are not to guide people to [the] right path. They merely express the enjoyment of some aspects of life which happen to be morally good. They give you some outlook upon life which has a vastness that transcends all ordinary purposes of life and stirs [the] imagination.

His role as an early intermediary between the East and the West cannot be underestimated. Tagore's most recent biographers summarize the years of his most profound poetry in this precise way:

> Like some other highly educated Bengalis of his time, until about 1920 Tagore believed British rule in India to be providential, necessary for the reform of a moribund, degenerate society. But as a patriot, particular-

ly after 1900, he needed to believe in the persistence of ancient India's spiritual values in contemporary India.... [T]hrough his poems *Gitanjali ...* and through his personal presence in England—where people were even reminded of Christ—these two beliefs became harmonized in his mind. For a few brief years he brought East and West into receptive emotional and intellectual contact. Thereafter, with the First World War, the upsurge of the Indian nationalist movement, its suppression by the imperial government, and the popularity of the non-cooperation movement led by Gandhi, neither belief proved tenable. Both, however, continued to coexist in Tagore's mind.... As a direct consequence, he found himself obliged to defend Indian spirituality when abroad, and the spirit of the West when in India. Not surprisingly he felt inwardly torn and often tortured.[1]

Tagore's mysticism, as seen in his most important poetry from these years before the First World War, is the subject of this small book.

Tagore did not title his poems; the editor has added descriptive titles here. The poems have also been reorganized from their original published sequence. After each title, a small number appears in parentheses; these numbers are for readers who may want to cross-reference to the original editions of *The Gardener* and *Gitanjali,* in which the numbers were the only organizing principle.

A Short Introduction to Tagore's Mysticism

The civilizations evolved in India or China, Persia or Judaea, Greece or Rome are like several mountain peaks having different altitude, temperature, flora and fauna, and yet belonging to the same chain of hills.

—RABINDRANATH TAGORE, FROM *THE RELIGION OF MAN*

At a symposium commemorating the 125th anniversary of the birth of Rabindranath Tagore, Mother Teresa of Calcutta said: "There's something very very beautiful in Rabindranath: his heart, his tender love for God. He loved God. And he has written some beautiful songs. Two or three of them we sing in our chapel during our prayers. There's one of them—*'E jibon punyo koro'* ('Sanctify our lives with love')—to be able to love, we need a clean heart, an empty heart that can be filled with God's love. He had a tender love for people. And he put that love into action by writing beautiful things about God, about people, about nature; and he expressed that tender love continually."[2]

Rabindranath Tagore's spiritual vision is embodied in all of his work—novels, plays, and paintings—but especially in his poetry. He had the ability to speak to people of many backgrounds and spiritualities in simple ways. His verse is not difficult to understand or to enter into. However, all of his writing is, as he himself put it, filled "with the ancient spirit of India as revealed in our sacred texts and manifested in the life of today" (*Sadhana*, p. vii). There is a great deal of meaning behind some of his simple phrasings of love, devotion, and struggle for personal understanding.

The inner-seeking spirituality of India infused all of Tagore's writing. He wrote in many genres of the deep religious milieu of Hinduism. This passage from his novel *The Home and the World*, for instance, offers a domesticated version of the devotion so common in the spiritual feelings and actions of the Indian people:

> I know, from my childhood's experience, how devotion is beauty itself, in its inner aspect. When my mother arranged the different fruits, carefully peeled by her own loving hands, on the white stone plate, and gently waved her fan to drive away the flies while my father sat down to his meals, her service would lose itself in a beauty which passed beyond outward forms. Even in my infancy I could feel its power. It transcended all debates, or doubts, or calculations: it was pure music.

The values and core beliefs of the Hindu scriptures permeated his work. These core beliefs include:

- The universe in which we live is a partial

manifestation of the Infinite Spirit.
- There is no hard and fast line between nature and humankind or between humankind and God. Evil and suffering are not absolute realities, but are only the temporary expedients of the evolving Spirit.
- The Absolute Spirit is all ineffable joy and love.
- True knowledge is that which perceives the unity of all things in God.
- The emancipation of humankind consists in our absolute self-surrender in service and love.[3]

His favorite of the Upanishads, which were the most philosophic of the ancient Vedantic texts of Hinduism, was the Isa Upanishad. William Radice, one of the most important of Tagore's interpreters today, writes: "The Isa Upanishad had been a revelation to his father, the religious reformer Debendranath Tagore, who describes in his autobiography how he found the first verse of the text by chance, on a loose page of a Sanskrit book fluttering past him.... It attempts through its contradictions to describe the interplay of world and spirit, eternal and temporal, infinite and finite, transcendent and immanent which Tagore himself defined as the main subject of all his writings."[4]

Rabindranath Tagore knew the following translation by the British scholar F. Max Müller. Despite its use of exclusive male pronouns, common until very recently in the scripture translations of all religious traditions, the Isa Upanishad still speaks from the depths of Indian spirituality. [Note: The brackets in this translation of the complete Isa Upanishad include clarifying words and phrases from the translator.]

The Isa Upanishad

1. All this, whatsoever moves on earth, is to be hidden in the Lord [the Self]. When thou hast surrendered all this, then thou mayest enjoy. Do not covet the wealth of any man!
2. Though a man may wish to live a hundred years, performing works, it will be thus with him; but not in any other way: work will thus not cling to a man.
3. There are the worlds of the Asuras covered with blind darkness. Those who have destroyed their self [who perform works, without having arrived at a knowledge of the true Self], go after death to those worlds.

4. That one [the Self], though never stirring, is swifter than thought. The Devas [senses] never reached it; it walked before them. Though standing still, it overtakes the others who are running. Matarisvan [the wind, the moving spirit] bestows powers on it.

5. It stirs and it stirs not; it is far, and likewise near. It is inside of all this, and it is outside of all this.

6. And he who beholds all beings in the Self, and the Self in all beings, he never turns away from it.

7. When to a man who understands, the Self has become all things, what sorrow, what trouble can there be to him who once beheld that unity?

8. He [the Self] encircled all, bright, incorporeal, scatheless, without muscles, pure, untouched by evil; a seer, wise, omnipresent, self-existent, he disposed all things rightly for eternal years.

9. All who worship what is not real knowledge [good works] enter into blind darkness: those who delight in real knowledge, enter, as it were, into greater darkness.

10. One thing, they say, is obtained from real knowledge; another, they say, from what is not knowledge. Thus we have heard from the wise who taught us this.

11. He who knows at the same time both knowledge and not-knowledge, overcomes death through not-knowledge, and obtains immortality through knowledge.

12. All who worship what is not the true cause enter into blind darkness: those who delight in the true cause, enter, as it were, into greater darkness.

13. One thing, they say, is obtained from [knowledge of] the cause; another, they say, from [knowledge of] what is not the cause. Thus we have heard from the wise who taught us this.

14. He who knows at the same time both the cause and the destruction [the perishable body], overcomes death by destruction [the perishable body], and obtains immortality through [knowledge of] the true cause.

15. The door of the True is covered with a golden disk. Open that, O Pushan, that we may see the nature of the True.

16. O Pushan, only seer, Yama [judge],

Surya [sun], son of Pragapati, spread thy rays and gather them! The light that is thy fairest form, I see it. I am what He is [viz. the person in the sun].

17. Breath to air, and to the immortal! Then this my body ends in ashes. Om! Mind, remember! Remember thy deeds! Mind, remember! Remember thy deeds!

18. Agni, lead us on to wealth [beatitude] by a good path, thou, O God, who knowest all things! Keep far from us crooked evil, and we shall offer thee the fullest praise!

In a series of lectures delivered in America and in England in 1913, Tagore attempted to explain his mysticism more deeply to the thousands of people in the West who were now reading his poetry. These lectures were published under the title *Sadhana: The Realization of Life* (see selections on pp. 27–29 below). Ernest Rhys, a contemporary listener to these talks and a good friend of Tagore, explains the mysticism of the poet and his poems:

Rabindranath brings his series of realizations to a period with his pages on the mystery of love. "Who could have breathed or moved if the sky were not filled with joy, with love?" The soul is on a pilgrimage: it is traveling from the law, which assigns its relative place in the moral order, to love, which is its moral freedom. Buddha named this infinite love *Brahma Vihara*—"the joy of living in Brahma." And he taught that whoever would attain to it must purge himself from hatred, and the malice of deceit, and the rage of injury. The free spirit was he who could have measureless love for all creatures—even as a mother has it for her only child.

The light within, the little ether in the heart, is continually flowing out to join the light without: it is the water-drop going to the sea, the child to the mother, the eye to the sun. Thus is fulfilled the circle of realizations. "From joy are born all creatures, by joy they are sustained, toward joy they progress, and into joy they enter." With this perfecting of the circle of delight our whole being dilates; a luminous consciousness of the far greater world about us enters the soul, and obsesses it. Then it is, indeed, that our spirit finds its larger self, and becomes sure it is immortal. "It dies a hundred times in its enclosures of self; for separateness is doomed to die, it cannot be made eternal. But it never can die where it is one with the all." There is the secret of that persuasion of immortality, which is instinctive in most of us, with the instinct of life itself and the obstinate desire for its perpetuity. Now convert the term of joy into love, and you have the lyric formula complete, which was behind the songs of the Vaishnava poets and is behind those of *Gitanjali*. "From love the world is born, by love it is sustained, toward love it moves, and into love it enters."

Tagore's mystical approach to living was also fed by tremendous sorrow in his personal life. Over the space of only five years, in the middle of the first decade of the twentieth century, Rabindranath's wife and two of his children, a boy and a girl, each thirteen years old, died. His three other children moved away from the family home; two daughters married and his other son went off to college in America. Tagore turned these tragedies and the resulting loneliness into great depths of spiritual insight. He saw these happenings in a much broader context than his own life; his own life, in fact, had no boundaries. "He sought God not merely in the privacy of his soul," writes one critic who worked with Tagore for several years, "but in every manifestation of [God's] play in the outside world."[5] Sadness and gaiety, beauty and tragedy, all were held in the life of God among us, according to Tagore's mystical perspective.

In the poems of *The Gardener* and *Gitanjali* that follow, we glimpse these spiritual perspectives, and much more. Ernest Rhys, one of Tagore's first biographers, offers one of the best summaries:

> If *The Gardener* is the song-book of youth and the romance of the young lover who is satisfied with a

flower for itself, or for its token of love's happiness, to be realized on earth in a day or night, *Gitanjali* is the book of the old lover who is in love with heavenly desire. He cannot be satisfied, but must always wish to transcend life and sensation through death, and attain not *Nirvana* in the sense of extinction, but *Brahma Vihara,* the joy eternal, the realization of love in its last abode.

One of his most perceptive critics describes the poems of *Gitanjali* further, explaining the different levels of meaning to be found there:

This indeed is the keystone of [Tagore's] spiritual philosophy or intuition—he will see God within himself and also permeating everything in the Universe, big or small, but not as a Super-Entity remote and self-isolated, luring [people] away from this world…. And so even in his most intensely religious and God-conscious mood, he would not turn away from life and this world. "Deliverance is not for me in renunciation. I feel the embrace of freedom in a thousand bonds of delight." Love is not the antithesis of duty; on the contrary, it relieves duty of its burden and makes what was dreary pleasurable. Love of God and love of the people are complementary and justify and fulfill each other.[6]

Excerpts from W. B. Yeats's
Introduction to *Gitanjali*

The great English poet of the twentieth century William Butler Yeats first introduced Tagore's work to readers in the West when he wrote the introduction to the first English-language edition of *Gitanjali*. In one remarkable, unbroken paragraph, Yeats enthused to his fellow readers before the First World War:

> I have carried the manuscript of these translations about with me for days, reading it in railway trains, or on the top of omnibuses and in restaurants, and I have often had to close it lest some stranger would see how much it moved me. These lyrics—which are in the original, my Indians tell me, full of subtlety of rhythm, of untranslatable delicacies of color, of metrical invention—display in their thought a world I have dreamed of all my life long. The work of a supreme culture, they yet appear as much the growth of the common soil as the grass and the rushes. A tradition, where poetry and religion are the same thing, has passed through the centuries, gathering from learned and unlearned metaphor and emotion, and carried back again to the multitude the thought of the scholar and of the noble. If the civilization of Bengal remains unbroken, if that common mind which—as one divines—runs through all, is not, as with us, bro-

ken into a dozen minds that know nothing of each other, something even of what is most subtle in these verses will have come, in a few generations, to the beggar on the roads…. These verses will not lie in little well-printed books upon ladies' tables, who turn the pages with indolent hands that they may sigh over a life without meaning, which is yet all they can know of life, or be carried about by students at the university to be laid aside when the work of life begins, but as the generations pass, travelers will hum them on the highway and men rowing upon rivers. Lovers, while they await one another, shall find, in murmuring them, this love of God a magic gulf wherein their own more bitter passion may bathe and renew its youth. At every moment the heart of this poet flows outward to these without derogation or condescension, for it has known that they will understand; and it has filled itself with the circumstance of their lives. The traveler in the red-brown clothes that he wears that dust may not show upon him, the girl searching in her bed for the petals fallen from the wreath of her royal lover, the servant or the bride awaiting the master's homecoming in the empty house, are images of the heart turning to God. Flowers and rivers, the blowing of conch shells, the heavy rain of the Indian July, or the parching heat, are images of the moods of that heart in union or in separation; and a man sitting in a boat upon a river playing upon a lute, like one of those figures full of mysterious meaning in a Chinese picture, is God himself. A whole people, a whole civilization, immeasurably strange to us, seems to have been taken up into this imagination; and yet we are not moved because of its strangeness, but because we have met our own image, as though we had walked in Rossetti's willow wood, or heard, perhaps for the first time in literature, our voice as in a dream.

Yeats continues, explaining some of the reasons why Tagore's work caught fire in the imaginations of so many readers in the West, where traditional forms of Christian spirituality that were in great need of refreshing dominated the imagination, in the early decades of the twentieth century:

Since the Renaissance the writing of European saints—however familiar their metaphor and the general structure of their thought—has ceased to hold our attention. We know that we must at last forsake the world, and we are accustomed in moments of weariness or exaltation to consider a voluntary forsaking; but how can we, who have read so much poetry, seen so many paintings, listened to so much music, where the cry of the flesh and the cry of the soul seem one, forsake it harshly and rudely? What have we in common with St. Bernard covering his eyes that they may not dwell upon the beauty of the lakes of Switzerland, or with the violent rhetoric of the Book of Revelation? We would, if we might, find, as in this book, words full of courtesy. "I have got my leave. Bid me farewell, my brothers! I bow to you all and take my departure.... A summons has come and I am ready for my journey." And it is our own mood, when it is furthest from à Kempis or John of the Cross, that cries, "And because I love this life, I know I shall love death as well." Yet it is not only in our thoughts of the parting that this book fathoms all. We had not known that we loved God, hardly it may be that we believed in Him.... This is no longer the sanctity of the cell and of the scourge; being but a lifting up, as it were, into a greater intensity of the mood of the painter, painting the dust and the sunlight, and we go for a like voice to St. Francis and to William Blake who have seemed so alien in our violent history.

Excerpts from Tagore's Prose Mystic Writings

The World of Personality

There is a point where in the mystery of existence contradictions meet; where movement is not all movement and stillness is not all stillness; where the idea and the form, the within and the without, are united; where infinite becomes finite, yet not losing its infinity. If this meeting is dissolved, then things become unreal.

When I see a rose leaf through a microscope, I see

it in a more extended space than it usually occupies for me. The more I extend the space the more it becomes vague. So that in the pure infinite, it is neither rose leaf nor anything at all. It only becomes a rose leaf where the infinite, reaches finitude at a particular point. When we disturb that point toward the small or the great, the rose leaf begins to assume unreality.

It is the same with regard to time.... One can be sure that there are things in this world which are known by other creatures, but which, since their time is not synchronous with ours, are nothing to us. The phenomenon that a dog perceives as a smell does not keep its time with that of our nerves, therefore it falls outside our world.

[Science] tries to do away altogether with that central personality, in relation to which the world is a world. Science sets up an impersonal and unalterable standard of space and time that is not the standard of creation. Therefore at its fatal touch the reality of the world is so hopelessly disturbed that it vanishes in an abstraction where things become nothing at all. For the world is not atoms and molecules or radioactivity or other forces, the diamond is not carbon, and light is not vibrations of ether. You can never come to the reality of creation by contemplating it from the point of view of destruction. Not only the world but also God is divested of reality by science, which subjects him to analysis in the laboratory of reason outside our personal relationship and then describes the result as unknown and unknowable. It is a mere tautology to say that God is unknowable, when we leave altogether out of account the person who can and who does know him. It is the same thing as saying that food is uneatable when the eater is absent.

—FROM *PERSONALITY* (1917)

Sectarianism and the Living

When we come to believe that we are in possession of our God because we belong to some particular sect it gives us such a complete sense of comfort, that God is needed no longer except for quarreling with others whose idea of God differs from ours in theoretical details.

Having been able to make provision for our God in some shadow land of creed we feel free to reserve all the space for ourselves in the world of reality, ridding it of the wonder of the Infinite, making it as trivial as our own household furniture. Such unlimited vulgarity only becomes possible when we have no doubt in our minds that we believe in God while our life ignores him.

The pious sectarian is proud because he is confident of his right of possession of God. The [person] of devotion is meek because he is conscious of God's right of love over his life and soul. The object of our possession becomes smaller than ourselves, and without acknowledging it in so many words the bigoted sectarian has an implicit belief that God can be kept secured for certain individuals in a cage which is of their own make.… Sectarianism is a perverse form of worldliness in the disguise of religion; it breeds a narrowness of heart in a greater measure than the cult of the world based upon material interest can ever do. For undisguised pursuit of self has its safety in its openness, like filth exposed to the sun and air. But the self-magnification with its consequent lessening of God that goes on unchecked under the cover of sectarianism loses its chance of salvation because it defiles the very source of purity.

Religion, like poetry, is not a mere idea, it is expression. The self-expression of God is in the endless variety of creation; and our attitude toward the Infinite Being must also in its expression have a variety of individuality ceaseless and unending. Those sects, which jealously build their boundaries with too rigid creeds excluding all spontaneous movement of the living spirit, may hoard their theology but they kill religion.

—FROM *THOUGHT RELICS* (1921)

The Indian Spiritual Worldview

Some modern philosophers of Europe, who are directly or indirectly indebted to the Upanishads, far from realizing their debt, maintain that the Brahma of India is a mere abstraction, a negation of all that is in the world. In a word, that the Infinite Being is to be found nowhere except in metaphysics. It may be, that such a doctrine has been and still is prevalent with a section of our countrymen. But this is certainly not in accord with the pervading spirit of the Indian mind. Instead, it is the practice of realizing and affirming the presence of the Infinite in all things that has been its constant inspiration.

We are enjoined to see "whatever there is in the world as being enveloped by God."

"I bow to God over and over again who is in fire and in water, who permeates the whole world, who is in the annual crops as well as in the perennial trees."

Can this be God abstracted from the world? Instead, it signifies not merely seeing him in all things, but saluting him in all the objects of the world. The attitude of the God-conscious [person] of the Upanishad toward the universe is one of a deep feeling of adoration. His object of worship is present everywhere. It is the one living truth that makes all realities true. This truth is not only of knowledge but also of devotion. "Namonamah," we bow to him everywhere, and over and over again. It is recognized in the outburst of the Rishi, who addresses the whole world in a sudden ecstasy of joy: "Listen to me, ye sons of the immortal spirit, ye who live in the heavenly abode, I have known the Supreme Person whose light shines forth from beyond the darkness." Do we not find the overwhelming delight of a direct and positive experience where there is not the least trace of vagueness or passivity?

Buddha, who developed the practical side of the teaching of Upanishads, preached the same message when he said, "With everything, whether it is above or below, remote or near, visible or invisible, thou shalt preserve a relation of unlimited love without any animosity or without a desire to kill. To live in such a consciousness while standing or walking, sitting or lying down till you are asleep, is *Brahma Vihara*, or, in other words, is living and moving and having your joy in the spirit of Brahma."

What is that spirit? The Upanishad says, "The being who is in his essence the light and life of all, who is world-conscious, is Brahma." To feel all, to be conscious of everything, is his spirit. We are immersed in his consciousness body and soul. It is through his consciousness that the sun attracts the earth; it is through his consciousness that the light-waves are being transmitted from planet to planet.

Not only in space, but "this light and life, this all-feeling being is in our souls." He is all-conscious in space, or the world of extension; and he is all-conscious in soul, or the world of intention.

Thus to attain our world-consciousness, we have

to unite our feeling with this all-pervasive infinite feeling. In fact, the only true human progress is coincident with this widening of the range of feeling. All our poetry, philosophy, science, art, and religion are serving to extend the scope of our consciousness toward higher and larger spheres.

—FROM *SADHANA: THE REALIZATION OF LIFE* (1913)

According to the true Indian view, our consciousness of the world, merely as the sum total of things that exist, and as governed by laws, is imperfect. But it is perfect when our consciousness realizes all things as spiritually one with it, and therefore capable of giving us joy. For us the highest purpose of this world is not merely living in it, knowing it and making use of it, but realizing our own selves in it through expansion of sympathy; not alienating ourselves from it and dominating it, but comprehending and uniting it with ourselves in perfect union.

—FROM *CREATIVE UNITY* (1922)

A Spiritual Education

Children are living beings—more living than grown-up people who have built shells of habit around themselves. Therefore it is absolutely necessary for their mental health and development that they should not have mere schools for their lessons, but a world whose guiding spirit is personal love. It must be an ashram where [people] have gathered for the highest end of life, in the peace of nature; where life is not merely meditative, but fully awake in its activities; where [children's] minds are not being perpetually drilled into believing that the ideal of the idolatry of the nation is the truest ideal for them to accept; where they are bidden to realize [humankind's] world as God's Kingdom to whose citizenship they have to aspire; where the sunrise and sunset and the silent glory of stars are not daily ignored; where nature's festivities of flowers and fruit have their joyous recognition from [humanity]; and where the young and the old, the teacher and the student, sit at the same table to take their daily food and the food of their eternal life.

Religion is not a fractional thing that can be doled out in fixed weekly or daily measures as one among various subjects in the school syllabus. It is the truth of our complete being, the consciousness of our personal relationship with the infinite; it is the true center of gravity of our life. This we can attain during our childhood by daily living in a place where the truth of the spiritual world is not obscured by a crowd of necessities assuming artificial importance; where life is simple, surrounded by fullness of leisure, by ample space and pure air and profound peace of nature; and where [people] live with a perfect faith in the eternal life before them.

—FROM *THOUGHTS FROM TAGORE* (1929)

East Meets West

I have been fortunate in coming into close touch with individual men and women of the western countries, and have felt with them their sorrows and shared their aspirations. I have known that they seek the same God, who is my God—even those who deny him. I feel certain that, if the great light of culture were extinct in Europe, our horizon in the East will mourn in darkness. It does not hurt my pride to acknowledge that, in the present age, western humanity has received its mission to be the teacher of the world; that her science, through the mastery of laws of nature, is to liberate human souls from the dark dungeon of matter. For this very reason I have realized all the more strongly, on the other hand, that the dominant collective idea in the western countries is not creative. It is ready to enslave or kill individuals, to drug a great people with soul-killing poison, darkening their whole future with the black mist of stupefaction, and emasculating entire races of men to the utmost degree of helplessness. It is wholly wanting in spiritual power to blend and harmonize; it lacks the sense of the great personality of [humankind].

The most significant fact of modern days is this, that the West has met the East. Such a momentous meeting of humanity, in order to be fruitful, must have in its heart some great emotional idea, generous and creative. There can be no doubt that God's choice has fallen upon the knights-errant of the West for the service of the present age; arms and armor have been given to them; but have they yet realized in their hearts the single-minded loyalty to their cause which can resist all temptations of bribery from the devil? The world today is offered to the West. She will destroy it, if she does not use it for a great creation of [humankind]. The materials for such a creation are in the hands of science; but the creative genius is in [humanity's] spiritual ideal.

Earnestly I ask the poet of the western world to realize and sing to you with all the great power of music which he has, that the East and the West are ever in search of each other, and that they must meet not merely in the fullness of physical strength, but in fullness of truth; that the right hand, which wields the sword, has need of the left, which holds the shield of safety.

The East has its seat in the vast plains watched over by the snow-peaked mountains and fertilized by rivers carrying mighty volumes of water to the sea. There, under the blaze of a tropical sun, the physical life has bedimmed the light of its vigor and lessened its claims. There [humanity] has had the repose of mind that has ever tried to set itself in harmony with the inner notes of existence. In the silence of sunrise and sunset, and on star-crowded nights, he has sat face to face with the Infinite, waiting for the revelation that opens up the heart of all that there is.

The [person] from the East, with his faith in the eternal, who in his soul had met the touch of the Supreme Person—did he never come to you in the West and speak to you of the Kingdom of Heaven? Did he not unite the East and the West in truth, in the unity of one spiritual bond between all children of the Immortal, in the realization of one great Personality in all human persons?

Yes, the East did once meet the West profoundly in the growth of her life. Such union became possible, because the East came to the West with the ideal that is creative, and not with the passion that destroys moral bonds. The mystic consciousness of the Infinite, which she brought with her, was greatly needed by the [people] of the West to give [them] balance.

On the other hand, the East must find her own balance in science—the magnificent gift that the West can bring to her. Truth has its nest as well as its sky. That nest is definite in structure, accurate in law of construction; and though it has to be changed and rebuilt over and over again, the need of it is never-ending and its laws are eternal. For some centuries the East has neglected the nest building of truth. She has not been attentive to learn its secret. Trying to cross the trackless infinite, the East has relied solely upon her wings. She has spurned the earth, till, buffeted by storms, her wings are hurt and she is tired, sorely needing help. But has she then to be told that the messenger of the sky and the builder of the nest shall never meet?

—FROM *CREATIVE UNITY* (1922)

The Mystical Meaning of Life's Journey

The question is asked, if life's journey were endless where is its goal? The answer is, it is everywhere. We are in a palace which has no end, but which we have reached. By exploring it and extending our relationship with it we are ever making it more and more our own. The infant is born in the same universe where lives the adult of ripe mind. But its position is not like a [schoolchild] who has yet to learn his alphabet, finding himself in a college class. The infant has its own joy of life because the world is not a mere road, but a home, of which it will have more and more as it grows up in wisdom. With our road the gain is at every step, for it is the road and the home in one; it leads us on yet gives us shelter.

A block of stone is unplastic, insensitive, and inert; it offers resistance to the creative idea of the artist. But for a sculptor its very obstacles are an advantage and he carves his image out of it. Our physical existence is an obstacle to our spirit, it has every aspect of bondage, and to all appearance it is a perpetual humiliation to our soul. And therefore it is the best material for our soul to manifest her through it, to proclaim her freedom by fashioning ornaments out of her fetters. The limitations of our outer circumstances are only to give opportunities to our soul, and by being able to defy them she realizes her truth.

—FROM THOUGHT RELICS (1921)

Poems from
The Gardener

Into a Larger Existence (61)

Peace, my heart,
let the time for the parting be sweet.
Let it not be a death but completeness.
Let love melt into memory and pain into songs.
Let the flight through the sky end
in the folding of the wings over the nest.
Let the last touch of your hands
be gentle like the flower of the night.
Stand still,
O Beautiful End,
for a moment,
and say your last words in silence.
I bow to you and hold up my
lamp to light you on your way.

A Sanskrit poem admired by Tagore:
    For the family, sacrifice the individual.
    For the community, the family.
    For the country, the community.
    For the soul, all the world.

Conversation between Friends (27)

"Trust love even if it brings sorrow.
Do not close up your heart."
"Ah no, my friend, your words are dark, I can-
not understand them."

"The heart is only for giving away with a tear
and a song, my love."
"Ah no, my friend, your words are dark, I can-
not understand them."

"Pleasure is frail like a dewdrop, while it laughs
it dies.
But sorrow is strong and abiding. Let sorrowful
love wake in your eyes."
"Ah no, my friend, your words are dark, I can-
not understand them."

"Spiritual freedom consists in the arousal of a cosmic con-
sciousness through 'Bodher Sadhana' (the practice of sensi-
tivity) through which the self comes out of itself and is spiri-
tually aware of its kinship not only with the human world,
but also with the animal and even with the inanimate world.
In a joyous state of mind [we see ourselves] in all beings and
all beings in [ourselves]. This is the realization of the
'Brahma' in the finite individual."—Arati Sen[7]

"The lotus blooms in the sight of the sun, and
  loses all that it has.
It would not remain in bud in the eternal winter
  mist."
"Ah no, my friend, your words are dark, I can-
  not understand them."

Preparing for a Guest *(10)*

Let your work be, bride.
Listen, the guest has come.
Do you hear, he is gently shaking the chain
    which fastens the door?
See that your anklets make no loud noise, and
    that your step is not over-hurried at meeting
    him.
Let your work be, bride,
the guest had come in the evening.

No, it is not the ghostly wind, bride,
do not be frightened.
It is the full moon on a night of April;
shadows are pale in the courtyard; the sky
    overhead is bright.
Draw your veil over your face if you must,
carry the lamp to the door if you fear.
No, it is not the ghostly wind, bride,
do not be frightened.

Have no word with him if you are shy;
stand aside by the door when you meet him.
If he asks you questions, and if you wish to,
you can lower your eyes in silence.
Do not let your bracelets jingle when, lamp in
    hand,
you lead him in.

Have no words with him if you are shy.

Have you not finished your work yet, bride?
Listen, the guest has come.
Have you not lit the lamp in the cowshed?
Have you not got ready the offering basket for
the evening service?
Have you not put the red lucky mark at the part-
ing of your hair,
and done your toilette for the night?
O bride, do you hear, the guest has come?
Let your work be!

True Wealth *(74)*

In the world's audience hall, the simple blade of
    grass sits on the same carpet with the sun-
    beam and the stars of midnight.
Thus my songs share their seats in the heart of
    the world with the music of the clouds and
    forests.
But, you man of riches, your wealth has no part
    in the simple grandeur of the sun's glad gold
    and the mellow gleam of the musing moon.
The blessing of the all-embracing sky is not shed
    upon it.
And when death appears, it pales and withers
    and crumbles into dust.

What Is Boundless and Endless (28)

Your questioning eyes are sad. They seek to
    know my meaning as the moon would fath-
    om the sea.
I have bared my life before your eyes from end
    to end, with nothing hidden or held back.
    That is why you know me not.
If it were only a gem, I could break it into a
    hundred pieces and string them into a chain
    to put on your neck.
If it were only a flower, round and small and
    sweet, I could pluck it from its stem to set it
    in your hair.
But it is a heart, my beloved. Where are its
    shores and its bottom?
You know not the limits of this kingdom, still
    you are its queen.
If it were only a moment of pleasure it would
    flower in an easy smile, and you could see it
    and read it in a moment.
If it were merely a pain it would melt in limpid
    tears, reflecting its inmost secret without a
    word.
But it is love, my beloved.
Its pleasure and pain are boundless, and endless
    its wants and wealth.
It is as near to you as your life, but you can
    never wholly know it.

Don't Go *(34)*

Do not go, my love,
without asking my leave.
I have watched all night,
and now my eyes are heavy with sleep.
I fear lest I lose you when I'm sleeping.
Do not go, my love,
without asking my leave.

I start up and stretch my hands to touch you.
I ask my self, "Is it a dream?"
Could I but entangle your feet with my heart
    and hold them fast to my breast!
Do not go, my love, without asking my leave.

Longings of Love (41)

I long to speak the deepest words I have to say
    to you;
but I dare not, for fear you should laugh.
That is why I laugh at myself and shatter my
    secret in jest.
I make light of my pain, afraid you should do
    so.

I long to tell you the truest words I have to say
    to you;
but I dare not, being afraid that you would not
    believe them.
That is why I disguise them in untruth,
saying the contrary of what I mean.
I make my pain appear absurd, afraid that you
    should do so.

I long to use the most precious words I have for
    you;
but I dare not, fearing I should not be paid with
    like value.
That is why I give you hard names and boast of
    my callous strength.
I hurt you, for fear you should never know any
    pain.

I long to sit silent by you;

but I dare not lest my heart come out at my lips.
That is why I prattle and chatter lightly and hide
   my heart behind words.
I rudely handle my pain, for fear you should do
   so.

I long to go away from your side;
but I dare not, for fear my cowardice should
   become known to you.
That is why I hold my head high and carelessly
   come into your presence.
Constant thrusts from your eyes keep my pain
   fresh forever.

Spirit Touch (49)

I hold her hands and press her to my breast.
I try to fill my arms with her loveliness,
to plunder her sweet smile with kisses,
to drink her dark glances with my eyes.
Ah, but, where is it?
Who can strain the blue from the sky?
I try to grasp the beauty; it eludes me,
leaving only the body in my hands.
Baffled and weary I come back.
How can the body touch the flower which only
    the spirit may touch?

Friends (78)

It was in May.
The sultry noon seemed endlessly long.
The dry earth gaped with thirst in the heat.
When I heard from the riverside a voice calling,
"Come, my darling!"
I shut my book and opened the window to look
out.
I saw a big buffalo with mud-stained hide stand-
ing
near the river with placid, patient eyes; and a
youth,
knee-deep in water, calling it to its bath.
I smiled amused and felt a touch of sweetness in
my heart.

A Heaven Too Narrow (44)

Reverend sir, forgive this pair of sinners.
Spring winds today are blowing in wild eddies,
   driving dust and dead leaves away, and with
   them your lessons are all lost.
Do not say, father, that life is a vanity.
For we have made truce with death for once,
   and only for a few fragrant hours we two
   have been made immortal.

Even if the king's army came and fiercely fell
   upon us we should sadly shake our heads
   and say, Brothers, you are disturbing us. If
   you must have this noisy game, go and clatter
   your arms elsewhere. Since only for a few
   fleeting moments we have been made immor-
   tal.

If friendly people came and flocked around us,
   we should humbly bow to them and say, This
   extravagant good fortune is an embarrassment
   to us. Room is scarce in the infinite sky
   where we dwell. For in the springtime flowers
   come in crowds, and the busy wings of bees
   jostle each other. Our little heaven, where
   dwell only we two immortals, is too absurdly
   narrow.

Let Your Life Lightly Dance (45)

To the guests that must go bid God's speed
and brush away all traces of their steps.
Take to your bosom with a smile what is easy
and simple and near.
Today is the festival of phantoms that know not
when they die.
Let your laughter be but a meaningless mirth
like twinkles of light
on the ripples.
Let your life lightly dance on the edges of Time
like dew
on the tip of a leaf.
Strike in chords from your harp fitful momentary
rhythms.

I Raised a Temple (72)

With days of hard travail I raised a temple. It
  had no doors or windows, its walls were
  thickly built with massive stones.
I forgot all else, I shunned all the world, I gazed
  in rapt contemplation at the image I had set
  upon the altar.
It was always night inside, and lit by the lamps
  of perfumed oil.
The ceaseless smoke of incense wound my heart
  in its heavy coils.
Sleepless, I carved on the walls fantastic figures
  in mazy bewildering lines—winged horses,
  flowers with human faces, women with limbs
  like
  serpents.
No passage was left anywhere through which
  could enter the song birds, the murmur of
  leaves, or hum of the busy village.
The only sound that echoed in its dark dome
  was that of incantations which I chanted.
My mind became keen and still like a pointed
  flame, my sense swooned in ecstasy.
I knew not how time passed till the thunder-
  stone had struck the temple, and a pain stung
  me through the heart.

The lamp looked pale and ashamed; the carv-
     ings on the walls, like chained dreams, stared
     meaningless in the light as they would fain
     hide themselves.
I looked at the image on the altar. I saw it smil-
     ing and alive with the living touch of God.
     The
     night I had imprisoned had spread its wings
     and vanished.

You Ask (26)

"What comes from your willing hands I take. I
  beg for nothing more."
"Yes, yes, I know you, modest mendicant, you
  ask for all that one has."

"If there be a stray flower for me I will wear it in
  my heart."
"But if there be thorns?"
"I will endure them."
"Yes, yes, I know you, modest mendicant, you
  ask for all that one has."

"If but once you should raise your loving eyes to
  my face it would make my life sweet beyond
  death."
"But if there be only cruel glances?"
"I will keep them piercing my heart."
"Yes, yes, I know you, modest mendicant, you
  ask for all that one has."

A Silent Guest (4)

Ah me, why did they build my house
by the road to the market town?
They moor their laden boats near my trees.
They come and go and wander at their will.
I sit and watch them; my time wears on.
Turn them away I cannot. And thus my days
    pass by.

Night and day their steps sound by my door.
Vainly I cry, "I do not know you."
Some of them are known to my fingers, some to
    my nostrils,
the blood in my veins seems to know them,
and some are known to my dreams.
Turn them away I cannot.
I call them and say, "Come to my house whoev-
    er chooses.
Yes, come."
In the morning the bell rings in the temple.
They come with their baskets in their hands.
Their feet are rosy red. The early light of dawn is
    on their faces.
Turn them away I cannot. I call them and I say,
"Come to my garden to gather flowers. Come
    hither."

In the mid-day the gong sounds at the palace
    gate.

I know not why they leave their work and
linger near my hedge.
The flowers in their hair are pale and faded;
the notes are languid in their flutes.
Turn them away I cannot. I call them and say,
"The shade is cool under my trees. Come,
    friends."

At night the crickets chirp in the woods.
Who is it that comes slowly to my door and
    gently knocks?
I vaguely see the face, not a word is spoken,
the stillness of the sky is all around.
Turn away my silent guest I cannot.
I look at the face through the dark, and hours of
    dreams pass by.

Let's Squander Our Morning (84)

Over the green and yellow rice-fields sweep the
shadows of the autumn clouds followed by
the swift-chasing sun.
The bees forget to sip their honey; drunken with
light they foolishly hover and hum.
The ducks in the islands of the river clamor in
joy for mere nothing.
Let none go back home, brothers, this morning,
let none go to work.
Let us take the blue sky by storm and plunder
space as we run.
Laughter floats in the air like foam on the flood.
Brothers, let us squander our morning in futile
songs.

Madman Like a Tree Uprooted (66)

A wandering madman was seeking the touch-
stone, with matted locks, tawny and dust-
laden, and body worn to a shadow, his lips
tight-pressed, like the shut-up doors of his
heart, his burning eyes like the lamp of a
glow-worm seeking its mate.

Before him the endless ocean roared.
The garrulous waves ceaselessly talked of hid-
den treasures, mocking the ignorance that
knew not their meaning.
Maybe he now had no hope remaining, yet he
would not rest, for the search had become his
life,—
Just as the ocean for ever lifts its arms to the sky
for the unattainable—
Just as the stars go in circles, yet seeking a goal
that can never be reached—
Even so on the lonely shore the madman with
dusty tawny locks still roamed in search of
the
touchstone.

One day a village boy came up and asked, "Tell
me, where did you come at this golden chain
about your waist?"
The madman started—the chain that once was
iron was verily gold; it was not a dream, but

he did not know when it had changed.
He struck his forehead wildly—where, O where
    had he without knowing it achieved success?
It had grown into a habit, to pick up pebbles
    and touch the chain, and to throw them away
    without looking to see if a change had come;
    thus the
    madman found and lost the touchstone.
The sun was sinking low in the west, the sky
    was of gold.
The madman returned on his foot-steps to seek
    anew the lost treasure, with his strength
    gone, his body bent, and his heart in the
    dust, like a tree uprooted.

A Traveler's Wishes (63)

Traveler, must you go?
The night is still and the darkness swoons upon
  the forest.
The lamps are bright in our balcony, the flowers
  all fresh, and the youthful eyes still awake.
Is the time for your parting come?
Traveler, must you go?

We have not bound your feet with our entreat-
  ing arms.
Your doors are open. Your horse stands saddled
  at the gate.
If we have tried to bar your passage it was but
  with our songs.
Did we ever try to hold you back it was but with
  our eyes.
Traveler, we are helpless to keep you. We have
  only our tears.

What quenchless fire glows in your eyes?
What restless fever runs in your blood?
What call from the dark urges you?
What awful incantation have you read among
  the stars in the sky, that with a sealed secret
  message the night entered your heart, silent
  and strange?

If you do not care for merry meetings, if you
    must have peace, weary heart, we shall put
    our lamps out and silence our harps.
We shall sit still in the dark in the rustle of
    leaves, and the tired moon will shed pale rays
    on your window.
O traveler, what sleepless spirit has touched you
    from the heart of the midnight?

Why Does That Happen? *(52)*

Why did the lamp go out?
I shaded it with my cloak to save it from the
 wind,
that is why the lamp went out.

Why did the flower fade?
I pressed it to my heart with anxious love,
that is why the flower faded.

Why did the stream dry up?
I put a dam across it to have it for my use,
that is why the stream dried up.

Why did the harp-string break?
I tried to force a note that was beyond its power,
that is why the harp-string is broken.

Following Me at Day's End

The day is not yet done, the fair is not over,
the fair on the river-bank.
I had feared that my time had been
squandered and my last penny lost.
But no, my brother, I have still something left.
My fate has not cheated me of everything.

The selling and buying are over.
All the dues on both sides have been gathered
    in,
and it is time for me to go home.
But, gatekeeper, do you ask for your toll?
Do not fear, I have still something left.
My fate has not cheated me of everything.

The lull in the wind threatens storm,
and the lowering clouds in the west bode no
    good.
The hushed water waits for the wind.
I hurry to cross the river before the night over-
    takes me.
O ferryman, you want your fee!
Yes, brother, I have still something left.
My fate has not cheated me of everything.

In the wayside under the tree sits the beggar.
Alas, he looks at my face with a timid hope!
He thinks I am rich with the day's profit.

Yes, brother, I have still something left.
My fate has not cheated me of everything.
The night grows dark and the road lonely.
Fireflies gleam among the leaves.
Who are you that follow me with stealthy silent
    steps?
Ah, I know, it is your desire to rob me of all my
    gains.
I will not disappoint you!
For I still have something left, and my fate
has not cheated me of everything.

At midnight I reach home.
My hands are empty.
You are waiting with anxious eyes at my door,
sleepless and silent.
Like a timorous bird you fly to my breast with
    eager love.
Ay, ay, my God, much remains still.
My fate has not cheated me of everything.

Time for Flower Gathering (57)

I plucked your flower, O world!
I pressed it to my heart and the thorn pricked.
When the day waned and it darkened,
I found that the flower had faded,
but the pain remained.

More flowers will come to you with
perfume and pride, O world!
But my time for flower gathering is over,
and through the dark night I have not my rose,
only the pain remains.

Note from the Next Life ₍₈₅₎

Who are you, reader,
reading my poems a hundred years hence?
I cannot send you one single flower
from this wealth of spring,
one single streak of gold from yonder clouds.
Open your doors and look abroad.
From your blossoming garden gather fragrant
memories of the vanished flowers
of a hundred years before.
In the joy of your heart may you feel the living
    joy that
sang one spring morning, sending its
glad voice across a hundred years.

Through the Bars of a Cage (6)

The tame bird was in a cage,
the free bird was in the forest.
They met when the time came, it was a decree
    of fate.
The free bird cries, "O my love, let us fly to
    wood."
The cage bird whispers,
"Come hither, let us both live in the cage."
Says the free bird, "Among bars,
where is there room to spread one's wings?"
"Alas," cries the cage bird,
"I should not know where to sit perched in the
    sky."

The free bird cries, "My darling,
sing the songs of the woodlands."
The cage bird says, "Sit by my side,
I'll teach you the speech of the learned."
The forest bird cries, "No, ah no!
songs can never be taught."
The cage bird says "Alas for me,
I know not the songs of the woodlands."

Their love is intense with longing,
but they never can fly wing to wing.
Through the bars of the cage they look,

and vain is their wish to know each other.
They flutter their wings in yearning,
and sing, "Come closer, my love!"
The free bird cries, "It cannot be,
I fear the closed doors of the cage."
The cage bird whispers, "Alas,
my wings are powerless and dead."

Trouble with Intimacy (56)

I was one among many women busy with the
   obscure
daily tasks of the household.
Why did you single me out and bring me away
from the cool shelter of our common life?

Love unexpressed is sacred. It shines like gems
   in the gloom
of the hidden heart.
In the light of the curious day it looks pitifully
   dark.
Ah, you broke through the cover of my heart
   and dragged my trembling love into the open
   place, destroying forever the shady corner
   where it hid its nest.

The other women are the same as ever.
No one has peeped into their inmost being, and
   they themselves
know not their own secret.
Lightly they smile, and weep, chatter, and work.
Daily they go to the temple,
light their lamps,

and fetch water from the river.

I hoped my love would be saved from the shiv-
    ering shame
of the shelterless,
but you turn your face away.
Yes, your path lies open before you, but you
    have
cut off my return,
and left me stripped naked
before the world
with its lidless eyes
staring night and day.

Not Knowing (14)

I was walking by the road, I do not know why,
when the noonday was past and bamboo
    branches rustled in the wind.
The prone shadows with their out-stretched
    arms clung to
the feet of the hurrying light.
The *koels* were weary of their songs.
I was walking by the road, I do not know why.

The hut by the side of the water is shaded by
an overhanging tree.
Someone was busy with her work,
and her bangles made music in the corner.
I stood before this hut, I know not why.

The narrow winding road crosses many a mus-
    tard field,
and many a mango forest.
It passes by the temple of the village and the mar-
    ket at
the river landing-place.
I stopped by this hut, I do not know why.

Years ago it was a day of breezy March when
    the murmur
of the spring was languorous, and mango blos-
    soms were
dropping on the dust.
The rippling water leapt and licked the brass
vessel that stood on the landing-step.
I think of that day of breezy March, I do not
    know why.

Shadows are deepening and cattle returning to
    their folds.
The light is gray upon the lonely meadows,
and the villagers are waiting for the ferry at the
    bank.
I slowly return upon my steps, I do not know
    why.

A Fleeting Touch *(22)*

When she passed by me with quick steps,
the end of her skirt touched me.
From the unknown island
of a heart came a sudden
warm breath of spring.
A flutter of a flitting touch
brushed me and vanished in a moment,
like a torn flower petal
blown in the breeze.
It fell upon my heart
like a sigh of her body
and whisper of her heart.

Afterlife (2)

"Ah, poet, the evening draws near;
your hair is turning gray.
"Do you in your lonely musing hear the
message of the hereafter?"

"It is evening," the poet said,
"and I am listening because some one may call
from the village, late though it be.
"I watch if young straying hearts meet together,
and two pairs of eager eyes beg for music to
break their silence and speak for them.
"Who is there to weave their passionate songs,
if I sit on the shore of life and contemplate
    death and the beyond?

"The early evening star disappears.
"The glow of a funeral pyre slowly dies by the
    silent river.
"Jackals cry in chorus from the courtyard of the
    deserted house
    in the light of the worn-out moon.
"If some wanderer, leaving home, come here to
watch the night and with bowed head listen to
    the murmur
of the darkness, who is there
to whisper the secrets of life into his ears if I,
shutting my doors,
should try to free myself from mortal bonds?

"It is a trifle that my hair is turning gray.
"I am ever as young or as old as the youngest
and the oldest of this village.
"Some have smiles, sweet and simple,
and some a sly twinkle in their eyes.
"Some have tears that well up in the daylight,
and others tears that are hidden in the gloom.
"They all have need for me,
and I have no time to brood over the afterlife.
"I am of an age with each,
what matter if my hair turns gray?"

Poems from
Gitanjali
("Song Offerings")

Have You Not Heard His Silent Steps? <small>(45)</small>

Have you not heard his silent steps?
He comes, comes, ever comes.
Every moment and every age, every day and
    every
night he comes, comes, ever comes.
Many a song have I sung in many a mood of
    mind,
but all their notes have always proclaimed,
"He comes, comes, ever comes."
In the fragrant days of sunny April through the
    forest
path he comes, comes, ever comes.
In the rainy gloom of July nights on the thunder-
    ing
chariot of clouds he comes, comes, ever comes.
In sorrow after sorrow it is his steps that press
    upon my heart,
and it is the golden touch of his feet that makes
    my joy to shine.

Tagore does not always speak of God as a lover for whom

one longs. Intimacy with the Divine can also carry with it fear, anxiety, and self-doubt. Other poems from *Gitanjali*, below, express this feeling as well.

Let My Country Awake (35)

Where the mind is without fear
and the head is held high;
Where knowledge is free;
Where the world has not been broken up into
     fragments
by narrow domestic walls;
Where words come out from the depth of truth;
Where tireless striving stretches its arms toward
     perfection;
Where the clear stream of reason has not lost its
     way
into the dreary desert sand of dead habit;
Where the mind is led forward by thee into
     ever-widening
thought and action—
Into that heaven of freedom, my Father,
let my country awake.

"If a feeling lies deep in a poet's consciousness, it wants to give permanent form to itself through beauty of linguistic expression. Love adorns itself: it wants, through beauty, to prove externally the joy it carries within." —Rabindranath Tagore[8]

The Rain Has Held Back for Days (40)

The rain has held back for days and days,
my God, in my arid heart.
The horizon is fiercely naked—
not the thinnest cover of a soft cloud,
not the vaguest hint of a distant cool shower.
Send thy angry storm, dark with death,
if it is thy wish, and with lashes of lightning
startle the sky from end to end.
But call back, my lord,
call back this pervading silent heat,
still and keen and cruel,
burning the heart with dire despair.
Let the cloud of grace bend low from above
like the tearful look of the mother on the day of
    the father's wrath.

Break Open the Door (39)

When the heart is hard and parched up,
come upon me with a shower of mercy.
When grace is lost from life, come with a burst
    of song.
When tumultuous work raises its din on all sides
shutting me out from beyond, come to me, my
    lord of silence,
with thy peace and rest.
When my beggarly heart sits crouched,
shut up in a corner, break open the door, my
    king,
and come with the ceremony of a king.
When desire blinds the mind with delusion and
    dust,
O thou holy one, thou wakeful,
come with thy light and thy thunder.

Begging from Door to Door (50)

I had gone a-begging from door to door in the
    village path,
when thy golden chariot appeared in the dis-
    tance
like a gorgeous dream and I wondered who was
    this
King of all kings!
My hopes rose high and methought my evil days
were at an end, and I stood waiting for alms to be
    given
unasked and for wealth scattered on all sides in
    the dust.
The chariot stopped where I stood. Thy glance
fell on me and thou camest down with a smile.
I felt that the luck of my life had come at last.
Then of a sudden thou didst hold out thy right
    hand and say
"What hast thou to give to me?"
Ah, what a kingly jest was it to open thy palm to
    a beggar to beg!
I was confused and stood undecided, and then
    from my wallet
I slowly took out the least little grain of corn
    and gave it to thee.
But how great my surprise when at the day's end
    I emptied my
bag on the floor to find a least little grain of gold
among the poor heap. I bitterly wept and
    wished that I had had

the heart to give thee my all.

Thy Love for Me Still Waits *(32)*

By all means they try to hold me secure who
  love me in this world.
But it is otherwise with thy love which is greater
  than theirs,
and thou keepest me free.
Lest I forget them they never venture to leave
  me alone.
But day passes by after day and thou art not
  seen.
If I call not thee in my prayers,
if I keep not thee in my heart,
thy love for me still waits
for my love.

Fill Me with Your Music <small>(7)</small>

My song has put off her adornments.
She has no pride of dress and decoration.
Ornaments would mar our union;
they would come between thee and me;
their jingling would crowd thy whispers.
My poet's vanity dies in shame before thy sight.
O master poet, I have sat down at thy feet.
Only let me make my life simple and straight,
like a flute of reed for thee to fill with music.

Flood of Joy *(57)*

Light, my light, the world-filling light,
the eye-kissing light, heart-sweetening light!
Ah, the light dances, my darling,
at the center of my life; the light strikes, my dar-
    ling,
the chords of my love; the sky opens,
the wind runs wild,
laughter passes over the earth.
The butterflies spread their sails on the sea of
    light.
Lilies and jasmines surge up on the crest of the
    waves of light.
The light is shattered into gold on every cloud,
    my darling,
and it scatters gems in profusion.
Mirth spreads from leaf to leaf, my darling,
and gladness without measure.
The heaven's river has drowned its banks
and the flood of joy is abroad.

My Sacred Shrine (33)

When it was day they came into my house and
    said,
"We shall only take the smallest room here."
They said, "We shall help you in the worship of
your God and humbly accept only our share of
    his grace";
and then they took their seat in a corner and
    they sat quiet and meek.
But in the darkness of night I find they break
into my sacred shrine, strong and turbulent,
and snatch with unholy greed the
offerings from God's altar.

I Am Here to Sing (15)

I am here to sing thee songs. In this
hall of thine I have a corner seat.
In thy world I have no work to do; my useless
    life
can only break out in tunes without a purpose.
When the hour strikes for thy silent worship
at the dark temple of midnight, command me,
my master, to stand before thee to sing.
When in the morning air the golden harp is
    tuned,
honor me, commanding my presence.

Face to Face (76)

Day after day, O lord of my life, shall I stand
    before thee face to face?
With folded hands, O lord of all worlds,
shall I stand before thee face to face?
Under thy great sky in solitude and silence,
with humble heart shall I stand before thee face
    to face?
In this laborious world of thine, tumultuous with
    toil and with struggle,
among hurrying crowds shall I stand before thee
    face to face?
And when my work shall be done in this world,
O King of kings, alone and speechless
shall I stand before thee face to face?

Waiting to Give Myself Up *(17)*

I am only waiting for love to give myself up at
    last into his hands.
That is why it is so late and why I have been
    guilty of such omissions.
They come with their laws and their codes to
    bind me fast;
but I evade them ever,
for I am only waiting for love to give myself up
    at last into his hands.
People blame me and call me heedless; I doubt
    not they are right in their blame.
The market day is over and work is all done for
    the busy.
Those who came to call me in vain have gone
    back in anger. I am only
waiting for love to give myself up at last into his
    hands.

My Prayer (36)

This is my prayer to thee, my lord—strike,
strike at the root of penury in my heart.
Give me the strength lightly to bear my joys and
  sorrows.
Give me the strength to make my love fruitful in
  service.
Give me the strength never to disown the poor
  or bend my knees before insolent might.
Give me the strength to raise my mind high
  above daily trifles.
And give me the strength to surrender my
  strength to thy will with love.

Sacred Love (9)

O fool, to try to carry thyself upon thy own
    shoulders!
O beggar, to come to beg at thy own door!
Leave all thy burdens on his hands who can
    bear all,
and never look behind in regret.
Thy desire at once puts out the light from the
    lamp
it touches with its breath.
It is unholy—
take not thy gifts through its unclean hands.
Accept only what is offered by sacred love.

Things Rush On *(70)*

Is it beyond thee to be glad with the gladness of
    this rhythm?
to be tossed and lost and broken in the whirl of
    this fearful joy?
All things rush on, they stop not,
they look not behind, no power can hold them
    back,
they rush on.
Keeping steps with that restless, rapid music,
seasons come dancing and pass away—
colors, tunes, and perfumes pour in endless cas-
    cades
in the abounding joy that scatters and gives up
    and
dies every moment.

I Shrink to Give Up My Life *(77)*

I know thee as my God and stand apart—
I do not know thee as my own and come closer.
I know thee as my father and bow before thy
    feet—
I do not grasp thy hand as my friend's.
I stand not where thou comest down and
    ownest
    thyself
as mine, there to clasp thee to my heart and
    take thee
as my comrade.
Thou art the Brother amongst my brothers,
but I heed them not, I divide not my earnings
    with them,
thus sharing my all with thee.
In pleasure and in pain I stand not by the side of
    men,
and thus stand by thee. I shrink to give up my
    life, and thus
do not plunge into the great waters of life.

All My Senses *(103)*

In one salutation to thee, my God, let all my
    senses
spread out and touch this world at thy feet.
Like a raincloud of July hung low with its bur-
    den of
unshed showers let all my mind bend down at
    thy door
in one salutation to thee.
Let all my songs gather together their diverse
    strains into
a single current and flow to a sea of silence in
    one salutation to thee.
Like a flock of homesick cranes flying night and
    day back
to their mountain nests let all my life take its
    voyage
to its eternal home in one salutation to thee.

The Poet in Me—Part One *(37)*

I thought that my voyage had come to its end at
the last limit of my power—that the path before
   me was closed,
that provisions were exhausted and the time
   come
to take shelter in a silent obscurity.
But I find that thy will knows no end in me.
And when old words die out on the tongue,
   new melodies
break forth from the heart; and where the old
   tracks are lost,
new country is revealed with its wonders.

The Poet in Me—Part Two *(65)*

What divine drink wouldst thou have, my God,
from this overflowing cup of my life?
My poet, is it thy delight to see thy creation
through my eyes and to stand at the portals
of my ears silently to listen to thine own eternal
    harmony?
Thy world is weaving words in my mind and thy
    joy
is adding music to them. Thou givest thyself to
    me in love
and then feelest thine own entire sweetness in
    me.

Our King of the Fearful Night *(51)*

The night darkened. Our day's works had been
    done.
We thought that the last guest had arrived for
    the night and
the doors in the village were all shut. Only
    some said,
the king was to come. We laughed and said
    "No, it cannot be!"
It seemed there were knocks at the door and we
    said
it was nothing but the wind. We put out the
    lamps and lay down to sleep.
Only some said, "It is the messenger!" We
    laughed and said
"No, it must be the wind!"
There came a sound in the dead of the night.
    We sleepily
thought it was the distant thunder. The earth
    shook, the walls rocked,
and it troubled us in our sleep. Only some said,
    it was the sound of wheels.
We said in a drowsy murmur, "No, it must be
    the rumbling of clouds!"
The night was still dark when the drum sound-
    ed. The voice came
"Wake up! delay not!" We pressed our hands on
    our hearts and
shuddered with fear. Some said, "Lo, there is the
    king's flag!" We stood up on our feet and

cried, "There is no time for delay!"
The king has come—but where are lights, where
are wreaths?
Where is the throne to seat him? Oh, shame,
Oh utter shame!
Where is the hall, the decorations? Someone has
said,
"Vain is this cry! Greet him with empty hands,
lead him into thy rooms all bare!"
Open the doors, let the conch-shells be sound-
ed!
In the depth of the night has come the king of
our dark, dreary house.
The thunder roars in the sky. The darkness shud-
ders with lightning.
Bring out thy tattered piece of mat and spread it
in the courtyard.
With the storm has come of a sudden our king
of the fearful night.

My Beloved Comes (22)

In the deep shadows of the rainy July, with
    secret steps,
thou walkest, silent as night,
eluding all watchers.
Today the morning has closed its eyes, heedless
of the insistent calls of the loud east wind,
and a thick veil has been drawn over the
ever-wakeful blue sky.
The woodlands have hushed their songs, and
    doors
are all shut at every house.
Thou art the solitary wayfarer
in this deserted street.
Oh my only friend,
my best beloved,
the gates are open in my house—
do not pass by like a dream.

The Tune of Thee and Me (71)

That I should make much of myself and turn it
    on all sides,
thus casting colored shadows on thy radiance—
such is thy maya.
Thou settest a barrier in thine own being and
    then callest
thy severed self in myriad notes. This thy self-
    separation
has taken body in me.
The poignant song is echoed through all the sky
    in
many-colored tears and smiles, alarms and
    hopes;
waves rise up and sink again, dreams break and
    form.
In me is thy own defeat of self.
This screen that thou hast raised is painted with
    innumerable
figures with the brush of the night and the day.
    Behind it
thy seat is woven in wondrous mysteries of
    curves,
casting away all barren lines of straightness.
The great pageant of thee and me has over-
    spread the sky.
With the tune of thee and me all the air is
    vibrant, and all ages pass
with the hiding and seeking of thee and me.

Light and Shadow (68)

Thy sunbeam comes upon this earth of mine
   with
arms outstretched and stands at my door the
   livelong day
to carry back to thy feet clouds made of my
   tears and sighs and songs.

With fond delight thou wrappest about thy
starry breast that mantle of misty cloud, turning
   it into
numberless shapes and folds and coloring it
   with hues ever-changing.

It is so light and so fleeting, tender and tearful
   and dark;
that is why thou lovest it, O thou spotless and
   serene.
And that is why it may cover thy awful white
light with its pathetic shadows.

What It Is *(84)*

It is the pang of separation that spreads
    throughout the world
and gives birth to shapes innumerable in the
    infinite sky.

It is this sorrow of separation that gazes in
    silence
all night from star to star and becomes lyric
among rustling leaves in rainy darkness of July.

It is this overspreading pain that deepens into
    loves and desires,
into sufferings and joys in human homes; and this
    it is
that ever melts and flows in songs through my
    poet's heart.

Life of My Life (4)

Life of my life, I shall ever try to keep my body
   pure, knowing
that thy living touch is upon all my limbs.
I shall ever try to keep all untruths out from my
   thoughts, knowing
that thou art that truth which has kindled the
   light of reason in my mind.
I shall ever try to drive all evils away from my
   heart
and keep my love in flower, knowing
that thou hast thy seat in the inmost shrine of
   my heart.
And it shall be my endeavor to reveal thee in
   my actions, knowing
it is thy power gives me strength to act.

The Deathless, the Silent (100)

I dive down into the depth of the ocean of
    forms,
hoping to gain the perfect pearl of the formless.

No more sailing from harbor to harbor with
this my weather-beaten boat.
The days are long passed when
my sport was to be tossed on waves.

And now I am eager to die into the deathless.

Into the audience hall by the fathomless abyss
where swells up the music of toneless strings
I shall take this harp of my life.

I shall tune it to the notes of forever, and, when
it has sobbed out its last utterance, lay down
my silent harp at the feet of the silent.

A Heart to Conquer (99)

When I give up the helm I know that the time
  has come
for thee to take it. What there is to do will be
  instantly done.
Vain is this struggle.

Then take away your hands and silently put up
  with
your defeat, my heart, and think it your good for-
  tune to
sit perfectly still where you are placed.

These my lamps are blown out at every little
  puff of wind,
and trying to light them I forget all else again
  and again.

But I shall be wise this time and wait in the
  dark,
spreading my mat on the floor;
and whenever it is thy pleasure,
my lord,
come silently and take thy seat here.

The Delight of Senses (73)

Deliverance is not for me in renunciation. I feel
    the embrace
of freedom in a thousand bonds of delight.
Thou ever pourest for me the fresh draught of
thy wine of various colors and fragrance,
filling this earthen vessel to the brim.
My world will light its hundred different lamps
    with thy
flame and place them before the altar of thy
    temple.
No, I will never shut the doors of my senses.
The delights of sight and hearing and touch
will bear thy delight.
Yes, all my illusions will burn into illumination
    of joy,
and all my desires ripen into fruits of love.

A Final Gift *(66)*

She who ever had remained in the depth of my
    being, in
the twilight of gleams and of glimpses; she who
    never opened
her veils in the morning light, will be my last gift to
    thee,
my God, folded in my final song.

Words have wooed yet failed to win her;
persuasion has stretched to her its eager arms in
    vain.

I have roamed from country to country keeping her
    in
the core of my heart, and around her have risen and
    fallen the
growth and decay of my life.

Over my thoughts and actions, my slumbers and
    dreams,
she reigned yet dwelled alone and apart.

Many a man knocked at my door and asked for her
and turned away in despair.

There was none in the world who ever saw
her face to face, and she remained in her loneliness
waiting for thy recognition.

When the Creation Was New ₍₇₈₎

When the creation was new and all the stars
    shone in their first
splendor, the gods held their assembly in the sky
    and sang
"Oh, the picture of perfection! the joy unal-
    loyed!"

But one cried of a sudden—
"It seems that somewhere there is a break in the
    chain of light and
one of the stars has been lost."

The golden string of their harp snapped, their
    song stopped,
and they cried in dismay—
"Yes, that lost star was the best, she was the glory
    of all heavens!"

From that day the search is unceasing for her, and
    the cry
goes on from one to the other that in her the
    world has
lost its one joy!

Only in the deepest silence of night the stars
    smile
and whisper among themselves—
"Vain is the seeking! Unbroken perfection is over all!"

My Garden Is Full of Blossoms (81)

On many an idle day have I grieved over lost
    time.
But it is never lost, my lord.
Thou hast taken every moment of my life in
    thine own hands.

Hidden in the heart of things thou art nourishing
seeds into sprouts, buds into blossoms,
and ripening flowers into fruitfulness.

I was tired and sleeping on my idle bed and
    imagined
all work had ceased. In the morning I woke up
    and found
my garden full with wonders of flowers.

Time and No-Time *(82)*

Time is endless in thy hands, my lord. There is
    none
to count thy minutes.
Days and nights pass and ages bloom and fade
    like flowers.
Thou knowest how to wait.
Thy centuries follow each other perfecting
a small wildflower.
We have no time to lose, and having no time
    we must
scramble for our chances. We are too poor to be
    late.
And thus it is that time goes by while I give it to
every querulous man who claims it, and thine
    altar is
empty of all offerings to the last.
At the end of the day I hasten in fear lest thy
    gate be shut;
but I find that yet there is time.

All That Is Joy ₍₅₈₎

Let all the strains of joy mingle in my last song—

the joy that makes the earth flow over in the
    riotous excess of the grass,

the joy that sets the twin brothers, life and death,

dancing over the wide world,

the joy that sweeps in with the tempest, shaking
    and waking

all life with laughter,

the joy that sits still with its tears on the open red
    lotus of pain, and

the joy that throws everything it has upon the dust,

and knows not a word.

About the Translator

Rabindranath Tagore translated all of the poems in this book. He wrote them first in Bengali and then in English. His word choices were sometimes primitive in his translations, but these only seem to add to the spiritual universality and power of his verse.

Many other artists, writers, and scholars have translated Tagore's work: William Radice, a scholar teaching in London, most authoritatively, and Deepak Chopra, the spiritual teacher, most popularly.

He Is Me (30)

I came out alone on my way to my tryst. But who
is this that follows me in the silent dark?

I move aside to avoid his presence but I escape him
    not.
He makes the dust rise from the earth with his
    swagger;
he adds his loud voice to every word that I utter.

He is my own little self, my lord, he knows no
    shame;
but I am ashamed to come to thy door in his
    company.

While There Is Time (6)

Pluck this little flower and take it,
delay not! I fear lest it droop
and drop into the dust.

It may not find a place in thy garland,
but honor it with a touch of pain from thy
hand and pluck it. I fear lest the day end
before I am aware, and the time
of offering go by.

Though its color be not deep and its smell
be faint, use this flower in thy service
and pluck it while there is time.

Notes

1. Krishna Dutta and Andrew Robinson, *Rabindranath Tagore: The Myriad-Minded Man* (London: Bloomsbury, 1997), pp. 1–2.

2. Quoted in *Universality in Tagore: Souvenir of a Symposium on Rabindranath Tagore*, ed. Fr. Luciano Colussi (Calcutta, India: Nitika/Don Bosco, 1991), p. 14.

3. R. S. Sarma, *Renascent Hinduism* (Bombay: Bharatiya Vidya Bhavan, 1966), excerpted from his chapter on Tagore, p. 184. (Inclusive language added.)

4. William Radice, *Rabindranath Tagore: Selected Poems* (New York: Penguin Books, 1994), p. 17.

5. Krishna Kripalani, *Tagore: A Biography* (New York: Grove Press, 1962), p. 204.

6. Kripalani, *Tagore*, p. 182.

7. Arati Sen, "The Concept of Mukti," in *Universality in Tagore*, p. 98.

8. From the essay "Modern Poetry" in *Rabindranath Tagore: Particles, Jottings, Sparks—The Collected Brief Poems*, trans. William Radice (London: Angel Books, 2001), p. 175.

Index of Poems *(by title)*

Other Books in
The Mystic Poets Series

HAFIZ

Preface by
Andrew Harvey

HOPKINS

Preface by
Rev. Thomas Ryan, CSP

Forthcoming in the Series

HILDEGARD
WHITMAN

Printed in the USA
CPSIA information can be obtained
at www.ICGtesting.com
JSHW010225191223
53977JS00016B/424